KU-629-911

# THE GOOD
☆ **CAT** ☆
# FOOD
## GUIDE

ROSEMARY AND ANDREW GASSON
ILLUSTRATED BY ROBIN RAY

Chatto & Windus
LONDON

## AUTHORS' NOTE

All the foods tested here are of the high quality required of Cat Food.
This is a guide to taste, and other useful information such as
packaging, availability, etc. The Cat Foods in our Reports have, where
possible, been tested by several cats, and ratings given by experienced
cat owners according to our Paws & Claws rating system (p. 29).
Where scores differed, we have taken an average; where scores
differed dramatically we have re-tested. The Ratings and Human
Comments are made by cat owners who know their cats well and
understand their reactions.

Published in 1992 by
Chatto & Windus Ltd
20 Vauxhall Bridge Road
London SW1V 2SA

All rights reserved. No part of this publication may
be reproduced, stored in a retrieval system, or transmitted
in any form, or by any means, electronic, mechanical, photocopying,
recording or otherwise, without the prior permission
of the publisher.

A CIP catalogue record for this book is
available from the British Library

ISBN 0 7011 3977 3

Copyright © The Good Cat Food Guide Company Ltd
Rosemary Gasson, Andrew Gasson and Robin Ray have asserted their
right to be identified as the authors of this work

Photoset by Rowland Phototypesetting Ltd
Bury St Edmunds, Suffolk
Printed in Great Britain by
Butler and Tanner Ltd, Frome, Somerset

THE INSPECTORS

The Good Cat
Food Guide

# ACKNOWLEDGEMENTS

**FELINE FOOD PURVEYORS**
Armitage Pet Products
Asda Supermarkets
BP Nutrition
Budgen Stores
Effemex
Friskies
Gateway Foodmarkets
Greenfields
Iams Company
Kennelpak
Kingfisher Premier Foods
Marks & Spencer
Quaker Canada
Quaker UK
Royal Canin
Safeway Supermarkets
Sainsbury's Supermarkets
Spillers Foods
Tesco Supermarkets
Waitrose

**TEMPORARY INSPECTORS**
Patrick from Stockwell
Eliza from Tunbridge Wells

**INTERMOG COURIERS**
Elizabeth Aiken
Robert Albertson
Cindy Babski
Sissel Bjerke
Peter Bluff
François Bringer
John Cody
Andrew Day
Wim de Vos
Hugo Dunn-Meynell
David Fairweather
Joyce Ferder
Sarah Finnett
Heather Fowler
Rowland Fowles
Mark Fraser
Michael Gavshon
David Green
Gabriele Hemken
Jack Hershberg
Simon Jarvis
Louise Marchant
Lotti Mears
Vito Monaco
Jan Morgan
Doreen Mutschmann
Elizabeth Mychael
Shona Niven
Poala Pasquini
Barbara Perry
John Peters Sr
Giovanni Savino
Douglas Sefton
Patrick Starling
Andrew Stevenson
Martha Teichner
Stephan Thomas
Nicholas Turner

**OTHERS**
James Allcock BVSc., MRCVS
PFMA

# A FEW WORDS OF INTRODUCTION

## FROM HARRODS, THE CHIEF INSPECTOR
### *(with help from the Editors)*

T he Inspectors and Editors feel that it is both more exciting and much healthier for Felines to be adventurous eaters! This is much easier nowadays since there is such a large range of products to choose from. In the following pages we present reports on interesting new Cat Foods as well as many old favourites.

Research and tasting are conducted by a full-time Feline team of Inspectors who are trained to achieve common standards of judgement with as much objectivity as the field allows.

Our method of testing is very simple. We randomly allocate to each of our Inspectors a representative selection of foods from both large, well-known manufacturers and the smaller independents. Each food is tasted individually and rated on our 'Paws & Claws' Scale from 0 to 5. Where a food scores a minimum 0 or a maximum 5, its rating is confirmed by at least one other Inspector. In case of disagreement, the Chief Inspector adjudicates.

THIS GUIDE REMAINS INDEPENDENT IN ITS EDITORIAL SELECTION AND DOES NOT ACCEPT ADVERTISING OR PAYMENT FROM ANY CAT FOOD MANUFACTURERS. ALL THE CAT FOODS IN THIS GUIDE HAVE BEEN GENUINELY TESTED BY REAL CATS. ALL THE INFORMATION IN THE GUIDE WAS CORRECT AT THE TIME OF TESTING FOR BRAND NAME, FLAVOUR, PACK SIZE ETC, AND WAS TAKEN FROM THE LABELS OR MANUFACTURERS' FACT SHEETS.

The entries are listed in alphabetical order of brand name, irrespective of food type, manufacturer or country of origin.

Our Inspectors have noticed an enormous proliferation of brands and flavours. They report that some of these varieties appear to be mixtures just for their own sake and many have proved far less appetising than the more simple recipes. But all in all, Cat Food has come a long way since the original Kitekat (still going strong) was first introduced in 1939.

The Inspectorate has now been increased to 12 by a programme of Feline recruitment. In addition to our existing policy of yearly re-certification, Felines now require the Editors to undergo regular refresher courses in Cat Food identification. We now have the full complement of both Senior and Junior Inspectors, all properly equipped with radio-controlled collars and other modern technology.

During the year, alas, we lost Oscar, who took early retirement because of incipient Katzheimer's Disease – he could no longer remember what he'd eaten; and Heywood (he died with his mouth full) from Canada. As a mark of respect, we are including his last report, No. 35.

The following pages are intended to give all our Feline subscribers a flavour of food fare currently available, as well as offering guidance to Humans on the range of possible products.

But, our investigations continue . . .

# THE INTERNATIONAL FELINE

A s our Inspectors are based in the UK, we have gratefully enlisted the aid of Intermog Couriers to locate quality Cat Foods from every corner of the globe. Their brave quest for the ultimate Feline delicacy has shown interesting and widely varied results.

Many countries have a range nearly as diverse as the UK but several Third World areas would present serious difficulties to the traveller. The most familiar brand to British and Australasian Felines is the ubiquitous Whiskas. This has been discovered everywhere from Iceland to Saudi Arabia, so that the Feline taking a holiday in Majorca or Indonesia will feel gastronomically at home. Another world-wide brand is Snappy Tom which, although manufactured in Thailand, has been tested from Australia to the Gulf.

We must report on 'no go' areas for Felines. Cat Food has not been located in Moscow – or anywhere else in Eastern Europe. We also strongly advise Felines against travel to China. There are disturbing rumours, which we urge you not to ignore, of perfectly respectable Felines ending up as lunch in a Shanghai restaurant. Other danger areas appear to be Haiti, where you might end up at the wrong end of a black magic ceremony; and Arctic regions, where long-haired Felines could well lose their skins.

# WARNING TO TRAVELLERS: BEWARE THE MAFF

O ur Inspectors have had to make special arrangements for world-wide testing because of THE MAFF. They protect and control *all* Cat Foods containing meat and fish imported into the UK. They assure us that protection is in the best interests of both Felines and Humans and, before you argue with THE MAFF, remember Pickles, who went out for an Italian meal and never came back. We also have irrefutable evidence of Government collusion in their activities and the use of strong-arm vets to make their control absolute.

So what is THE MAFF? We can now reveal that it hides behind the name of the Ministry of Agriculture, Fisheries and Food!! A MAFF Licence *must* be obtained for all Cat Food brought into the UK. They won't give you one but you must have one! This is known as CATS 22. We would stress to both Felines and travellers that it is not permitted to bring in Cat Food from abroad.

### CONTRABAND CAT FOOD IS NOT ALLOWED

**Important** Don't forget your shots before travelling and remember it's going to take you six months to get back into the UK if you leave the country. Also, there is no Duty Free allowance for Cat Food.

# HARRODS
*(Chief Inspector)*

T hey call me sophisticated, serious and very bossy – but I am the Chief Inspector! Three-quarters Burmese, I have sleek black fur and an aura of elegance. I now weigh 10lbs, two more than before I started work on the Guide. But for a thirteen-year-old I am in good shape considering the strenuous nature of my work!

I like to keep in constant touch with my team by sitting on the answerphone, available to adjudicate on Cat Food queries. I relish the opportunity to sample foods from foreign parts.

I am often accused of being a Feline hypochondriac – although I do have a genuinely nervous stomach – but nothing prevents me from going out on a collar and lead, and I enjoy being chauffeur-driven from my London pied-à-terre to visit friends and get away from work.

**Favourite food:** Safeway's Gourmet Pilchards in Prawn Jelly; Top Form Savoury Treats; or that square-shaped coley in plastic food containers.

**Hobbies:** Listening to Radio 3 on my personal stereo; championing the cause of under-privileged Felines, and catnapping.

**Unusual eating:** Tinned garden peas; baked beans and sultanas.

# WILKIE
### *(Deputy Chief Inspector)*

I'm a smart, well-groomed, intelligent tabby, though at 14lbs I'm seriously overweight. I'm eight years old and live in a South London semi-detached mansion run almost entirely for my benefit. I like to think I'm a sharp operator and I can negotiate myself lunch at several houses along the street.

I nearly didn't get this job because of the reports – clever Felines never like to put anything in writing. What's more the Chief wouldn't let me eat the free samples I'd arranged and made me do my food testings blindfold.

**Favourite food:** Whiskas Supermeat – Turkey flavour; Marks & Spencer's Chicken in Jelly; or fresh pigeon.

**Hobbies:** Birdwatching and hunting; I enjoy eating out . . .

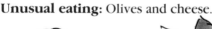

**Unusual eating:** Olives and cheese.

# ARNOLD
*(Chief Inspector – Retired)*

I am a mature Feline, of what might be considered a severely archaic disposition. Indeed, I am so old that I can remember the 'cat's meat man' from the days before manufactured Cat Foods were even thought of.

I have a gaunt appearance, with an Imperial weight of 7½lbs. The office of Chief Inspector, which I created, has been relinquished for this and subsequent editions of the Guide with more than a little reluctance. I still wished to contribute a few reports and have endeavoured to pen these with my customary attention to detail. I dislike both slang and modern brevity of language as well as most of the younger generation, whom I consider badly mannered and untidy eaters.

**Favourite food:** Freshly cooked coley but, where circumstances dictate a modern convenience food, my preference is for Friskies Gourmet Beef or Hi Life Sardines in Jelly.

**Hobbies:** Mainly sedentary, consisting of ornithology, television, and 'bowl watching' where I calculate the time interval between drips of the cold tap.

**Unusual eating:** Lightly scrambled egg.

# BASIL

I'm nine years old and doss in a 'bird and mouse' in Plaistow. They call me The Bruiser and they say I walk like John Wayne, 'cause I stick out all four feet at the same time – clever that. My fur's a bit moth-eaten, and I've got a cauliflower ear, from a territorial bout with Siamese Sid which I won paws down.

I may not be the brightest of Felines but my lady friends say my 'eart is in the right place 'cause I'll defend them and my territory to the bitter end. I'm a great believer in heducation, specially the two 'Rs' – raiding and rioting.

**Favourite foods:** Katkins Chunks with Kidney, which I can really get my last remaining tooth into; and Asda Quality Beef.

**Hobbies:** Lolling around street corners, and starting a good old-fashioned Feline rumble.

**Unusual eating:** Bread and butter; and crisps.

OUR INSPECTORS
# BENNETT

I'm the high-powered Feline achiever amongst the Inspectors. I live with a food and fitness fanatic in Norfolk and like to watch my weight, which is 8lbs, just right for my lean shape and size. I'm seven years old, with a short neat coat in a distinguished grey colour; by some quirk of nature my feet are white and 'trainer-like'.

I am very aware of what I eat and always try to get the correct nutritional balance in my diet. I normally refuse manufactured food but for the sake of the Guide I have broken my own rules. I try not to over-eat and often finish a meal with freshly cut grass, a renowned digestive aid for Felines. I also rely on homeopathic ingredients to complement a healthy diet and to assist the occasional minor ailment.

**Favourite food:** Denes Nature Cat, Rabbit and Chicken with Herbs (Additive Free); and Hill's Prescription Diet (obtainable from vets).

**Hobbies:** Healthy outdoor activities including long walks and chasing golf balls; indoors, wall-of-death racing in the bath tub whilst listening to classical music.

**Unusual eating:** Veggy burgers; cucumber.

# BORIS

I'm the original long-haired 'junkie' and live with an Oxford don who under my influence is now a real 'cool cat'.

My favourite turn-on is catnip which I often smuggle into the Senior Common Room disguised as an executive toy. I love those Feline 'E' numbers, especially the brand-loyalty ones which make me hyperactive. I've also been a pill addict for many years and eat brewer's yeast at an alarming rate. Anything small and round provides an irresistible attraction and I've tried overdosing on everything Human from Aspirin to cardiac pills. When the purr rises three octaves and the back legs splay, get the stomach pump ready!

I love getting stoned out of my tiny furry head and can be found – so the don says – purring fortissimo in the kitchen sink with my feet straight up in the air. The only addiction I won't try is smoking because of the risk of 'dog-ends'.

**Favourite food:** Liver, liver and liver. I sometimes need to be forcibly restrained from breaking into tins and eating more than is good for me.

**Hobbies:** I'm nearly always on another planet and have no time for hobbies.

**Unusual eating:** Kippers; and cream.

# JASMINE

As a nine-year-old tortoiseshell with delicate bone structure, short black and brown fur and a pretty face, I'm the sex kitten of the team. In my youth I was not above doing the odd spot of nude modelling for the centre-fold of one of the better-known Feline magazines.

Today, I keep my fur on but my reputation has ensured great popularity with the local toms. Despite this, I usually prefer the company of my Human with whom I can be very talkative in a one-sided sort of way.

I'm certainly not one of the 'Green' brigade and rather enjoy rearranging the anatomy of frogs and chasing the local squirrel. I also hate the next-door Feline bully and, although I regret it later, I have been known to lose both cool and femininity over this uncouth neighbour.

**Favourite food:** Purrfect Chicken and Turkey; Sainsbury's Supreme Selection Choice White Fish; or anything Humans eat.

**Hobbies:** Food lacrosse; and ornithology.

**Unusual eating:** Smoked turkey and the occasional curry.

# LUCIE 'N' FLOSSIE

Fascinating.

Utterly.

We are identical twins from Harrogate with short glossy fur. Talking isn't often necessary because we always know what the other is thinking. We are rather obsessive about our appearance and spend a lot of time on grooming while reminiscing in front of the mirror. Our nails are amongst our most attractive features and we have regular manicuring competitions on the kitchen wallpaper. They also come in useful for acupuncturing Humans. We prefer dry food as this is less likely to gum up our whiskers, but it is possible to tempt us with the occasional gourmet brand of wet food.

We are both getting on in years now and don't go out much, since we dislike all Felines except ourselves. We also have a touch of nervous agoraphobia and are worried by large birds. Indoors we don't do very much either. Once we were going to form an Indolence Society – but in the end we couldn't be bothered.

**Favourite food:** Meow Mix Beef, Liver and Heart; and Royal Canin C32 (Complete dry food).

**Hobbies:** Sleeping, grooming and spider-watching.

**Unusual eating:** Cheesecake.

OUR INSPECTORS
# NUTMEG

I'm a four-year-old Siamese tabby from the smart end of Aylesbury. They say I'm frightfully snobby but it's only to conceal a just slightly mixed ancestry. They sometimes make comments about my bronze colour but otherwise a petite frame and sleek body give me all the characteristics of the elegant Siamese. A secret not usually admitted is how my beautiful eyes are exactly the right colour with the aid of tinted contact lenses.

Despite a nervous disposition which is often mistaken for aloofness, I like to hang around the local stables and meet the huntin' set. They're a nicer class of Feline after all.

**Favourite food:** Friskies Gourmet Salmon à la Carte, though I say I like Black Cat Chicken – after all, it does have the Royal Warrant.

**Hobbies:** Learning buzz words from Human food guides; and nibbling the heads off flower arrangements.

**Unusual eating:** Dundee Cake and pasta.

# SAPHI

I'm just three years old and live in Bournemouth. Like many Felines of the younger generation I'm a member of the 'Green' lobby. I'm very careful what I eat and check that any manufactured food contains nothing nasty or environmentally unfriendly. I know I can't really become a vegetarian but try to avoid red meat whenever possible.

I also pay careful attention to packaging, always on the lookout for bio-degradable plastic pots or recycled paper cartons. Tins are disposed of in a safe place, preferably the 'can bank', and I've had the cat-flap double-glazed to conserve energy.

As a Green Feline, I do try not to upset the balance of nature too much when out huntin' and fishin'. Sometimes, though, I just don't know what comes over me and I feel a bit like Jekyll and Hyde when leaving indoor domesticity for an outdoor safari.

**Favourite food:** Hill's Feline Growth (Chicken and Maize); Tesco's Supreme Salmon and Tuna; and fresh-cut grass (fertilizer-free).

**Hobbies:** Newspaper shredding to make sure it's recycled.

**Unusual eating:** Sardines and ice-cream.

# TEDDY

I'm what you might call a film freak and my real-life hero is *Fritz the Cat*. I'm six years old and live in North London's Wood Green with some Norwegians. I call them *Aliens* while they call me *The Terminator* if I come home with a freshly caught bird. At 12lbs, I'm rather overweight because I take eating very seriously and then spend most of the time stretched out on top of the television set for *The Big Sleep*.

I find the language of films far more expressive than either English or Viking. Going out is *The Great Escape*; eating is always at *High Noon*; and I only talk to *Cat People* (1942 version). My favourite film is *Catablanca* and I can now purr to the tune of 'As time goes by'.

**Favourite food:** *Sheba* (1952 remake); and Brekkies – No. 007 on the Chief's Masterlist of Foods.

**Hobbies:** Watching films, and unravelling badly directed videos.

**Unusual eating:** Popcorn and Jarlsberg cheese.

Badly directed...

# THE FELINE FACT FILE

## SOME DEFINITIONS

**'Complete Foods'** contain all the nutrients necessary for a balanced Feline diet. They may include beneficial additives such as minerals and vitamins. Most prepared Cat Foods are complete.

**'Complementary Foods'** should only supplement Complete Foods since, however tasty, they are not nutritionally balanced. They include Treats and Human food.

Both complete and complementary foods should always be fed according to the directions on the label.

**'Flavour'**, **'Variety'** and **'With'** do not have the strict legal definitions of Human food in the UK. Good manufacturers include a substantial quantity of the named ingredient although it would be possible for this to be present as quite a small percentage.

Several foods from the same range could all consist of an identical main recipe. This explains why some fish varieties contain animal derivatives and *vice versa*. This 'core' recipe may vary from time to time (depending on the ingredients available) and could be the reason why perceptive Felines suddenly go off their favourite food.

## THE AVERAGE FELINE

Weighs 7–12lbs. 9lbs is a good average.

Needs 1 large or 2–3 small meals purr day.

Requires 400 calories purr day. (Equivalent to 400–500gm tinned or 125gm dry food.)

A large male should eat about 1 large tin purr day.

A small female should eat about ¾ of a large tin purr day.

Senior Felines (over 10) need 3–6 meals purr day with a total of 300–370gm.

## A GOOD DIET

**Must** contain animal protein (i.e. meat). Vegetable protein (e.g. soya) does not contain the necessary nutrients.

**Should** contain, on a moisture-free basis, 35–50% protein and 10–30% animal fat.

**Requires** a balance of at least 13 vitamins.

**Vitamin A** is most important – for night vision, correct weight, good skin and fertility – but avoid excess.

**Taurine** is an essential amino-acid.

**Fish oils** contain vitamin D3, essential for bone development – but avoid excess cod liver oil.

**Fluids** are essential. A loss of more than 10–15% of body fluids could be fatal. Some Felines don't appear to drink, but may obtain sufficient fluid from wet foods.

## MISCELLANEOUS DIET TIPS

Felines prefer food in lumps because of their teeth; they tear rather than chew.

Fish is best steamed or baked to preserve the nutrients. Be careful with bones.

It is natural to eat grass to help regurgitate fur balls (but regular combing should prevent their formation).

Dry foods help keep teeth free from tartar – but remember to give plenty of water.

The chlorine in fresh tapwater may irritate sensitive Feline noses.

Not all Felines like milk. Some are physically unable to digest it and end up with diarrhoea. However, a low-lactose variety is now available.

Catnip (catmint) is not addictive but it makes a Feline very happy.

**'Fat Cats' are fine – obese Felines are not!**

## AVOID . . .

Old or rancid food. It can make a Feline ill.

Chilled food (e.g. straight from the fridge). Felines prefer it at body temperature.

Small bones in poultry or rabbit (they become more brittle with cooking). Fish bones, if well cooked till definitely soft, can be safe and a good source of calcium.

Too little water relative to dry food – it could cause a urinary problem (NB: some specialised brands overcome this).

Too much liver – not more than 20% of a meal twice a week despite the addictive taste. Excess is dangerous because it causes problems with bones and joints.

Too much lean meat (e.g. pure steak with no fat). It could lead to calcium, iodine and Vitamin A deficiencies unless these are supplied separately.

Too many fish *fillets* (instead of meat). They can cause vitamin deficiencies. Whole fish is fine.

Raw fish. It should be cooked to destroy an unwanted enzyme which causes vitamin deficiency.

Raw egg, except in very small quantity. It neutralises other essential nutrients.

Dog food (Urrgh!). It contains insufficient protein for a routinely good Feline diet.

# FOOD TYPES

1 Convenient
2 Complete
3 Hygienic
4 Controlled
5 ⊗

**TINNED FOOD** *(Wet Food)*
Practical
Stores well
Tastier
Nutritious
Usually 'Complete'
May contain up to 80% water

Usually tastier...

WET

**DRY FOOD** *(Biscuits)*
Cheaper
Stores well
More pleasant to handle by Humans
Usually lower in fat
Contains little water (10%)
Fluid *must* be added to the diet
May contain salt to encourage drinking

**SEMI-MOIST/MOIST**
Nutritious
Can make up a large proportion of the diet
Stores well (but not as well as tinned)
Contains 20–30% water
Expensive
Usually low in fat
May contain significant *vegetable* protein

---

☆

---

# THE SYMBOLS &
# ABBREVIATIONS WE USE
## FOR MANUFACTURED CAT FOODS

### FOOD TYPE

WET

SEMI-MOIST/MOIST

DRY

### PACKAGING

TIN

BOX

FOIL

POT

OTHER

### AVAILABLE FROM

SUPERMARKET    (S)

MINI-MARKET    (M)

PETSHOP    (P)

OTHER    (O)
(e.g. Vet, Garden Centre, Petrol Station)

---

---

# KEY TO PAWS
# & CLAWS RATING

5 OUTSTANDING – A GASTRONOMIC DELIGHT

4 GOOD – DELICIOUS EATING

3 QUITE GOOD – TASTY EATING

2 VERY AVERAGE – BORING EATING

1 BELOW AVERAGE – ONLY EATEN WHEN DESPERATE

0 REFUSED TO EAT

In addition to the Paws & Claws Rating, 'Crossed Whiskers'

are awarded to Cat Foods of outstanding gastronomic interest – 'Recommended Eating'.

Cat Foods nominated for a Golden Whiskers Award (page 124–5) are marked with an asterisk.*

# FOOD REPORT No. 1

**BRAND NAME**    *Asda Quality*

**FLAVOUR**    *Salmon*

**PACKAGING**

**FOOD TYPE**

**MANUFACTURER**    *Asda Supermarkets*

**PACK SIZE** (gm)    *410gm*

**AVAILABLE FROM**    (S)  *Own label variety*

**NOTES**
*This is one of Asda's four own label ranges – Cat's Cuisine, Ocean Fayre, Quality Cat Food and Supreme. See Supplementary Reports below*

---

**INSPECTOR**    *Jasmine*

**INSPECTOR'S COMMENTS**
*More than magnificent – it's mediocre!*

**PAWS & CLAWS RATING**

**SUPPLEMENTARY REPORTS**
Cat's Cuisine: Beef, with Liver and Heart  *Harrods, 1*
Quality: Rabbit  *Teddy, 4*   Chicken  *Nutmeg, 2*
Supreme: Tuna  *Lucie 'N' Flossie, 2*
Ocean Fayre: Seafood Platter in Prawn Jelly  *Teddy, 5,*
    Sardines in Aspic  *Harrods, 4*

**HUMAN COMMENTS**
*She went off it after 2 minutes 11.3 seconds*

# FOOD REPORT NO. 2

BRAND NAME          *Black Cat*

FLAVOUR             *Beef and Liver*

PACKAGING

FOOD TYPE

MANUFACTURER        *BP Nutrition (UK)*

PACK SIZE (gm)      *400gm*

AVAILABLE FROM      (S)   (M)   (P)   (O)

NOTES
*Other flavours available*

---

INSPECTOR           *Nutmeg*

INSPECTOR'S COMMENTS
*What a disappointment . . . if only it had been
served* en croûte

PAWS & CLAWS RATING

SUPPLEMENTARY REPORTS
*Basil refused to eat the* Chicken *Flavour though
Nutmeg quite liked it*

HUMAN COMMENTS
*Very average, looks like pâté*

# FOOD REPORT No. 3

**BRAND NAME**     *Bonus*

**FLAVOUR**     *Fish/Meat*

**PACKAGING**

**FOOD TYPE**     

**MANUFACTURER**     *Spillers*

**PACK SIZE** (gm)     *400gm*

**AVAILABLE FROM**     (S)  (M)  (P)  (O)

**NOTES**
*Spillers other economy label is Savour Cat Food*

---

**INSPECTOR**     *Wilkie*

**INSPECTOR'S COMMENTS**
*Words fail me . . .*

**PAWS & CLAWS RATING**

**HUMAN COMMENTS**
*After the tasting Wilkie immediately went out for lunch*

# FOOD REPORT No. 4

BRAND NAME            *Brekkies*

FLAVOUR               *Pilchards*

PACKAGING

FOOD TYPE

MANUFACTURER          *Pedigree Petfoods*

PACK SIZE (gm)        *400gm and 1kg*

AVAILABLE FROM        (S)   (M)   (P)   (O)

NOTES
*A wide selection of flavours available*

---

INSPECTOR             *Harrods*

INSPECTOR'S COMMENTS
*Not a memorable meal. Personally I don't think fish
and biscuits go together*

PAWS & CLAWS RATING

SUPPLEMENTARY REPORTS
Chicken *received 3 from Teddy and Saphi awarded*
Rabbit *Flavour 2*

HUMAN COMMENTS
*Harrods treated it like a snack and didn't seem
satisfied until he had eaten a 'real' meal*

# FOOD REPORT NO. 5
## ISRAEL

**BRAND NAME**  *Catli*

**FLAVOUR**  *Meat and Liver*

**PACKAGING**

**FOOD TYPE**

**MANUFACTURER**  *Imported for Dogli*

**PACK SIZE** (gm)  *400gm*

**AVAILABLE FROM**  (S)

**NOTES**
*We couldn't understand why 'Chicken' was included in the list of contents when it's called Meat and Liver*

---

**INSPECTOR**  *Wilkie*

**INSPECTOR'S COMMENTS**
*Mazzeltov, just like chopped liver!*

**PAWS & CLAWS RATING**

**SUPPLEMENTARY REPORTS**
*Harrods and Jasmine both refused to eat Israeli* Bon Cat Food

**HUMAN COMMENTS**
*Good for Kosher cats*

# FOOD REPORT NO. 6

BRAND NAME                *Cats Choice*

FLAVOUR                   *Rabbit*

PACKAGING

FOOD TYPE

MANUFACTURER              *BP Nutrition (UK)*

PACK SIZE (gm)            *400gm*

AVAILABLE FROM            (S)  (M)  (P)  (O)

NOTES
*Comes in a 'four pack' of assorted flavours*

---

INSPECTOR                 *Basil*

INSPECTOR'S COMMENTS
*This was like the Venus de Milo . . . quite 'armless*

PAWS & CLAWS RATING

SUPPLEMENTARY REPORTS
Meat and Liver  *Wilkie, 3*
Salmon and Tuna  *Lucie 'N' Flossie, 1*
    *Teddy, 4*
Beef and Chicken  *Arnold, 3*

HUMAN COMMENTS
*The enthusiasm seemed to dwindle after the first
minute or two of eating*

# FOOD REPORT NO. 7
## NEW ZEALAND

**BRAND NAME**        *Chef*

**FLAVOUR**        *Chunky Chicken*

**PACKAGING**

**FOOD TYPE**

**MANUFACTURER**        *Bestfriend Petfoods*

**PACK SIZE** (gm)        *700gm*

**AVAILABLE FROM**        (S)

**NOTES**
*Preservative free*

---

**INSPECTOR**        *Nutmeg*

**INSPECTOR'S COMMENTS**
*Good Kiwi food. My compliments to the chef*

**PAWS & CLAWS RATING**

**HUMAN COMMENTS**
*She ate her way through an entire bowlful in one serious eating session*

# FOOD REPORT No. 8

**BRAND NAME**  *Choosy*

**FLAVOUR**  *Tuna*

**PACKAGING**

**FOOD TYPE**

**MANUFACTURER**  *Spillers*

**PACK SIZE** (gm)  *400gm*

**AVAILABLE FROM**  Ⓢ  Ⓜ  Ⓟ  Ⓞ

**NOTES**
*Choosy is also available in Superfish and Supermeat ranges*

---

**INSPECTOR**  *Boris*

**INSPECTOR'S COMMENTS**
*I'd get more of a buzz from reading the Oxford English Dictionary!*

**PAWS & CLAWS RATING**

**SUPPLEMENTARY REPORTS**
Salmon  *Teddy, 2*
  *Harrods, 2*
Chicken  *Harrods, 3*
Beef and Kidney  *Teddy, 1*

**HUMAN COMMENTS**
*Boris didn't show much enthusiasm for this, even though he was starving*

# FOOD REPORT NO. 9

**BRAND NAME**      *Co-op Supermeat*

**FLAVOUR**      *Salmon*

**PACKAGING**

**FOOD TYPE**

**MANUFACTURER**      *CWS*

**PACK SIZE** (gm)      *410gm*

**AVAILABLE FROM**      (S) *Own label variety*

**NOTES**
*Various basic flavours available*

---

**INSPECTOR**      *Basil*

**INSPECTOR'S COMMENTS**
*As pâté goes, not bad*

**PAWS & CLAWS RATING**

**SUPPLEMENTARY REPORTS**
Pilchards *Saphi, 2*
Beef *Nutmeg, 1*
Chicken *Teddy, 3*
Rabbit *Teddy, 0*

**HUMAN COMMENTS**
*For an economy range, this was fairly well received*

*Teddy didn't like the Rabbit*

# FOOD REPORT NO. 10

BRAND NAME  *Delikat*

FLAVOUR  *Real Beef*

PACKAGING  *Sachets packed in cardboard box*

FOOD TYPE

MANUFACTURER  *Quaker*

PACK SIZE (gm)  *170gm*

AVAILABLE FROM  (S) (M) (P) (O)

NOTES
*Several other flavours available in this range. (Hi Life Gourmet Complete Cat Food was the only other similar product found in the UK)*

---

INSPECTOR  *Lucie 'N' Flossie*

INSPECTOR'S COMMENTS
*It's a mystery how they get these real beefs into the sachets . . . but we did like it!*

PAWS & CLAWS RATING

SUPPLEMENTARY REPORTS
Rabbit *and* Fish *each rated 2 by Harrods*

HUMAN COMMENTS
*Handy packaging – no tin opener needed; also products stay fresh without a fridge*

*Basil quite liked Tender Beef*

# FOOD REPORT No. 11
## AUSTRALIA

**BRAND NAME**   *Dine*

**FLAVOUR**   *Salmon Pâté*

**PACKAGING**

**FOOD TYPE**

**MANUFACTURER**   *Uncle Ben's*

**PACK SIZE** (gm)   *180gm*

**AVAILABLE FROM**   (S)   (O)

**NOTES**
*Preservative free. Also available in Premium Dinner range*

---

**INSPECTOR**   *Teddy*

**INSPECTOR'S COMMENTS**
*I fell asleep with my face in the bowl*

**PAWS & CLAWS RATING**

**SUPPLEMENTARY REPORTS**
*Basil gave* Dine Tender Beef *a better rating of 3*

**HUMAN COMMENTS**
*I think he wanted to send it to Crocodile Dundee!*

# FOOD REPORT No. 12
## GERMANY

BRAND NAME            *Dokat*

FLAVOUR               *Fish*

PACKAGING              *Paper sack*

FOOD TYPE

MANUFACTURER          *Milkivit*

PACK SIZE (gm)        *400gm, 1.5kg, 5kg*

AVAILABLE FROM        (P)  (O)

NOTES
*One of three flavours – Meat and Vegetables, Fish and Chicken complete the range*

---

INSPECTOR             *Wilkie*

INSPECTOR'S COMMENTS
*Wunderbar! I always wanted to nominate an award*

PAWS & CLAWS RATING *

SUPPLEMENTARY REPORTS
*Our inspectors were unanimouse in their praise of* Dokat Dried Food. *Also tested in Germany:* Kitekat Beef *and* Whiskas Rabbit and Venison, *both rated 4*

HUMAN COMMENTS
*Wilkie couldn't get enough of Dokat and was constantly breaking into the packet*

# FOOD REPORT NO. 13

**BRAND NAME**  *Febo-Meowmix*

**FLAVOUR**  *Seafood, Shrimp and Tuna*

**PACKAGING**    *Paper sack*

**FOOD TYPE**

**MANUFACTURER**  *Febo Professional*

**PACK SIZE** (gm)  *200gm*

**AVAILABLE FROM**  (S) (P) (O)

**NOTES**
*Other flavours available in this range. Also sold loose
from petshops*

---

**INSPECTOR**  *Arnold*

**INSPECTOR'S COMMENTS**
*I do not usually indulge in dry food, but must
concede that this was exceptionally tasty*

**PAWS & CLAWS RATING**

**HUMAN COMMENTS**
*A surprising success for a traditional eater like
Arnold – in fact it was non-stop eating*

# FOOD REPORT No. 14

BRAND NAME                 *Feline Growth*

FLAVOUR                    *Chicken and Maize*

PACKAGING                  *Paper sack*

FOOD TYPE

MANUFACTURER               *Hill's Petfood Products*

PACK SIZE                  *4lb and 10lb bags*

AVAILABLE FROM             *Vets and* ◎

NOTES
*A concentrated formulation mainly for younger
Felines. Also available as Feline Maintenance for the
grown-up Feline*

---

INSPECTOR                  *Nutmeg*

INSPECTOR'S COMMENTS
*Simply brill . . .*

PAWS & CLAWS RATING
*Definitely recommended for 'younger' Felines*

SUPPLEMENTARY REPORTS
Feline Maintenance *was rated 3 by Saphi who suffered
exhaust problems afterwards*

HUMAN COMMENTS
*A good but expensive product. Should be served with
liquid refreshments*

57

# FOOD REPORT No. 15

BRAND NAME          *Felix Supreme*

FLAVOUR             *Duck and Heart*

PACKAGING

FOOD TYPE

MANUFACTURER        *Quaker*

PACK SIZE (gm)      *400gm*

AVAILABLE FROM      (S) · (M)  (P)  (O)

NOTES
*One of the more unusual flavour combinations from
Felix*

---

INSPECTOR           *Saphi*

INSPECTOR'S COMMENTS
*This tasted good enough to be a free-range duck*

PAWS & CLAWS RATING

SUPPLEMENTARY REPORTS
Chicken *Teddy, 1*
  *Lucie 'N' Flossie, 4*
Beef *Wilkie, 1*
Tuna *Arnold, 1   Nutmeg, 4*
Beef and Liver *Jasmine, 2*
Trout and Shrimp *Arnold, 4\**

HUMAN COMMENTS
*'Green' Saphi might have rated this even higher if the
tin had been recyclable*

# FOOD REPORT NO. 16
## FRANCE

BRAND NAME          *Fido*

FLAVOUR             *Saumon Truite*

PACKAGING

FOOD TYPE

MANUFACTURER        *Quaker France*

PACK SIZE (gm)      *200gm*

AVAILABLE FROM      (S)  (O)

NOTES
*One of at least deux autres flavours*

---

INSPECTOR           *Harrods*

INSPECTOR'S COMMENTS
*C'est magnifique!*

PAWS & CLAWS RATING  * 🐾 🐾 🐾 🐾 🐾

SUPPLEMENTARY REPORTS
*Other French varieties include* Friskies, Sheba, Ron Ron *and* Hourrah

HUMAN COMMENTS
*This is Harrods' all-time favourite. Canard au Foie came a very close second, but by unanimouse decision of all the inspectors, Saumon Truite won by a whisker*

Lamb + liver
= jolly good

# FOOD REPORT NO. 17

**BRAND NAME**  *Friskies Gourmet*

**FLAVOUR**  *Chicken and Kidney*

**PACKAGING**

**FOOD TYPE**

**MANUFACTURER**  *Friskies*

**PACK SIZE** (gm)  *185gm*

**AVAILABLE FROM**   (S)  (M)  (P)  (O)

**NOTES**
*This range also available in 390gm size as well as some good meat and fish combinations*

---

**INSPECTOR**  *Saphi*

**INSPECTOR'S COMMENTS**
*A heavenly combination, simple and unpretentious*

**PAWS & CLAWS RATING**

**SUPPLEMENTARY REPORTS**
A La Carte: Salmon *Jasmine, 2*  Bennett, 4,
    Beef *Harrods, 3*  Seafood *Boris, 4*
Gourmet Frisk: Seafood Platter in Prawn Jelly *Lucie
    'N' Flossie, 3*
Gourmet: Liver and Chicken *Saphi, 1,*
    Pilchards *Arnold, 5*  Beef and Rabbit *Harrods, 4,*
    Lamb and Liver *Harrods, 4*
    Rabbit *and* Fish *were each rated 2 by Harrods*

**HUMAN COMMENTS**
*Saphi was pleased with the small tin size because it
    avoided waste – a definite hit*

63

# FOOD REPORT NO. 18

**BRAND NAME**   *Gala*

**FLAVOUR**   *Meat and Fish*

**PACKAGING**

**FOOD TYPE**

**MANUFACTURER**   *BP Nutrition (UK)*

**PACK SIZE** (gm)   *400gm*

**AVAILABLE FROM**    (S) (M) (P) (O)

**NOTES**
*An economy brand*

---

**INSPECTOR**   *Wilkie*

**INSPECTOR'S COMMENTS**
*I retired to bed after this one, but then I often retire to bed*

**PAWS & CLAWS RATING**

**SUPPLEMENTARY REPORTS**
*Re-tests on this by Wilkie, Teddy and Harrods couldn't better this rating*

**HUMAN COMMENTS**
*Wilkie likes to know what he's eating!*

# FOOD REPORT NO. 19

**BRAND NAME**     *Go-Cat*

**FLAVOUR**     *Lamb and Beef*

**PACKAGING**     

**FOOD TYPE**     

**MANUFACTURER**     *Friskies*

**PACK SIZE** (gm)     *375gm*

**AVAILABLE FROM**     (S)  (M)  (P)  (O)

**NOTES**
*Several other flavours available*

---

**INSPECTOR**     *Teddy*

**INSPECTOR'S COMMENTS**
*I wish I'd tried this before. It really did taste like* The Lamb that Time Forgot

**PAWS & CLAWS RATING** *

**SUPPLEMENTARY REPORTS**
Go-Cat: Chicken and Turkey *Nutmeg, 3*
Go-Cat Special Blend: Tuna, Mackerel and Pilchards
    *Saphi, 4*
    Chicken, Duck and Turkey *Jasmine, 5 Crossed Whiskers*
    Duck, Rabbit and Beef *Basil, 3   Bennett, 2*

**HUMAN COMMENTS**
*A good crunchy snack which Teddy enjoyed*

# FOOD REPORT NO. 20
## AUSTRALIA

**BRAND NAME**  *Gourmet Delights*

**FLAVOUR**  *Tuna with Shrimp and Calamari*

**PACKAGING**

**FOOD TYPE**

**MANUFACTURER**  *Safcol*

**PACK SIZE** (gm)  *100gm*

**AVAILABLE FROM**  Ⓢ

**NOTES**
*Ring-pull can*

---

**INSPECTOR**  *Basil*

**INSPECTOR'S COMMENTS**
*Fair dinkum, sport*

**PAWS & CLAWS RATING**

**HUMAN COMMENTS**
*He liked this so much he was thinking about emigrating to Australia!*

Yum, (if I may be permitted the locution) yum.

# FOOD REPORT NO. 21

BRAND NAME             *Greenfields Chub Roll*

FLAVOUR               *Beef*

PACKAGING             *Sausage skin*

FOOD TYPE

MANUFACTURER          *Greenfields*

PACK SIZE (gm)        *907gm*

AVAILABLE FROM        (P)  (O)

NOTES
*A Complementary Food. Feline 'Salami' available in
assorted flavours. A similar type of product available
from Forthglade*

---

INSPECTOR             *Arnold*

INSPECTOR'S COMMENTS
*The underlying simplicity of this flavour
complemented a pleasantly aromatic texture, making
for a very substantial and excellent meal.
Recommended eating for a change*

PAWS & CLAWS RATING

HUMAN COMMENTS
*Arnold found this a nostalgic change from tinned
food. Also good value for money*

# FOOD REPORT NO. 22

**BRAND NAME** *Hi Life Gourmet*

**FLAVOUR** *Seafood Platter in Jelly*

**PACKAGING**

**FOOD TYPE**

**MANUFACTURER** *Pets Pantry*

**PACK SIZE** (gm) *185gm*

**AVAILABLE FROM** (S) (M) (P) (O)

**NOTES**
*Several flavours and sizes available in this mainly fishy range. Hi Life now have a Complete Moist Cat Food product in various flavours on the market, packed in individual sachets, similar to Delikat (Report No. 10)*

---

**INSPECTOR** *Lucie 'N' Flossie*

**INSPECTOR'S COMMENTS**
*We were amazed. It looked like fish . . . it tasted like fish and . . . it was fish!*

**PAWS & CLAWS RATING**

**SUPPLEMENTARY REPORTS**
Siamese Sardines in Jelly *Bennett, 3*
Sardines and Tuna Flakes *Harrods, 4*
Chopped Pilchards in Crab Jelly *Boris, 4\**
Turkey *Jasmine 3*
Tuna *Bennett, 5*
Pilchards in Jelly *Teddy, 4*

**HUMAN COMMENTS**
*The jelly was obviously the icing on the cake*

73

*Basil refused the Adult range*

# FOOD REPORT NO. 23

**BRAND NAME** *Iams for less active cats*

**FLAVOUR** *Chicken and Meat*

**PACKAGING** *Milk carton*

**FOOD TYPE**

**MANUFACTURER** *The Iams Company*

**PACK SIZE** (gm) *679gm*

**AVAILABLE FROM** (P) (O)

**NOTES**
*Range also includes products for junior and adult
Felines. Other sizes available are 3kg and 9kg*

---

**INSPECTOR** *Lucie 'N' Flossie*

**INSPECTOR'S COMMENTS**
*We think this food gives a new meaning to the word
'boredom'*

**PAWS & CLAWS RATING**

**SUPPLEMENTARY REPORTS**
*Nutmeg gave* Adult *4 but Basil refused to eat it*

**HUMAN COMMENTS**
*A well-intentioned but expensive product*

*Too rich for me...*

# FOOD REPORT NO. 24

**BRAND NAME**　　　　*Katkins Meat Loaf*

**FLAVOUR**　　　　　*Chicken and Turkey*

**PACKAGING**

**FOOD TYPE**

**MANUFACTURER**　　*Pedigree Petfoods*

**PACK SIZE** (gm)　　*400gm*

**AVAILABLE FROM**　　(S)　(M)　(P)　(O)

**NOTES**
*Katkins Chunks completes the range. Recyclable tin*

---

**INSPECTOR**　　　　*Nutmeg*

**INSPECTOR'S COMMENTS**
*Rather a rich combination for me and I felt rather queasy afterwards*

**PAWS & CLAWS RATING**

**SUPPLEMENTARY REPORTS**
Meat Loaf: Beef and Liver *Harrods, 2*
Chunks: Chicken *Wilkie, 5*　Rabbit *Harrods, 4*
　Beef *Arnold, 4*　*Jasmine, 3*

**HUMAN COMMENTS**
*She really did seem very queasy*

# FOOD REPORT NO. 25

**BRAND NAME**  *Kattomeat (Arthur's)*

**FLAVOUR**  *Salmon and Cod*

**PACKAGING**

**FOOD TYPE**

**MANUFACTURER**  *Spillers*

**PACK SIZE** (gm)  *185gm*

**AVAILABLE FROM**

**NOTES**
*A good choice of flavours available in Spillers' largest range. 185gm and 390gm sizes in recyclable tins*

---

**INSPECTOR**  *Boris*

**INSPECTOR'S COMMENTS**
*Man, this really set my whiskers vibrating!!*

**PAWS & CLAWS RATING**  *

**SUPPLEMENTARY REPORTS**
Chicken and Turkey  *Harrods, 2*
Salmon & Cod  *Harrods, 4*
Chicken and Liver  *Saphi, 5 Crossed Whiskers*
Rabbit and Chicken  *Lucie 'N' Flossie, 3*
Tuna and Sardine  *Jasmine, 3*
Turkey and Heart  *Harrods, 4\**

**HUMAN COMMENTS**
*He ate with happy relish and enthusiasm*

# FOOD REPORT NO. 26

BRAND NAME       *Kitekat*

FLAVOUR       *Pilchards*

PACKAGING      

FOOD TYPE      

MANUFACTURER       *Pedigree Petfoods*

PACK SIZE (gm)       *400gm*

AVAILABLE FROM       (S)   (M)   (P)   (O)

NOTES
*Supercrunch Dry, Tender Chunks and Supreme
Selection complete the range*

---

INSPECTOR       *Jasmine*

INSPECTOR'S COMMENTS
*Delicious, a real taste-bud teaser*

PAWS & CLAWS RATING      

SUPPLEMENTARY REPORTS
Kitekat: Pilchards *Boris, 4*   Liver *Saphi, 1*
    Chicken and Rabbit *Wilkie, 2*
Kitekat Tender Chunks: Beef *Basil, 4*
    Chicken *Boris, 3*

HUMAN COMMENTS
*She really ate her heart out over this one*

# FOOD REPORT NO. 27

**BRAND NAME**            *Kitekat Supercrunch*

**FLAVOUR**               *Liver and Game*

**PACKAGING**

**FOOD TYPE**

**MANUFACTURER**          *Pedigree Petfoods*

**PACK SIZE** (gm)        *300gm*

**AVAILABLE FROM**        (S)   (M)   (P)   (O)

**NOTES**
*One of two Kitekat Dry ranges*

---

**INSPECTOR**             *Arnold*

**INSPECTOR'S COMMENTS**
*An imaginative mix of flavours which succeeded in
maintaining my interest*

**PAWS & CLAWS RATING**

**SUPPLEMENTARY REPORTS**
*Wilkie rated* Kitekat Supreme Dry Selection Rabbit,
Lamb, Liver and Game *3*

**HUMAN COMMENTS**
*He quite enjoyed it. The flavour seemed more
interesting than usual*

# FOOD REPORT NO. 28

BRAND NAME — *Meow Mix*

FLAVOUR — *Shrimp, Tuna and Seafood*

PACKAGING —

FOOD TYPE —

MANUFACTURER — *Quaker*

PACK SIZE (gm) — *300gm*

AVAILABLE FROM —  Ⓢ Ⓜ Ⓟ Ⓞ

NOTES
*A Complementary Food. Also available in Beef, Liver and Heart variety*

INSPECTOR — *Basil*

INSPECTOR'S COMMENTS
*Wot a winner!*

PAWS & CLAWS RATING

SUPPLEMENTARY REPORTS
*Lucie 'n' Flossie gave this flavour 2 and Nutmeg 3*

HUMAN COMMENTS
*Looked good but smelled a bit salty. Basil needed a good long drink as it made him very thirsty*

*Lucie 'n' Flossie gave this a 2*

# FOOD REPORT NO. 29

BRAND NAME            *Nature Cat*

FLAVOUR              *Turkey and Lamb with Herbs*

PACKAGING

FOOD TYPE

MANUFACTURER         *Denes Natural Pet Food*

PACK SIZE (gm)       *400gm*

AVAILABLE FROM       (S)  (M)  (P)  (O)

NOTES
*No artificial flavours or colourings added. Recyclable
tin*

---

INSPECTOR            *Bennett*

INSPECTOR'S COMMENTS
*It may be healthy, but the nicest thing I can say
about this food is that the tin was round*

PAWS & CLAWS RATING

SUPPLEMENTARY REPORTS
Beef and Liver with Herbs  *Jasmine, 3*
Salmon and Tuna with Herbs  *Harrods, 2*
Chicken and Turkey with Herbs  *Nutmeg, 1*
Nature Kitten  *Boris, 2*

HUMAN COMMENTS
*Not a great success according to our health freak*

*The Chief adjudicates*

# FOOD REPORT NO. 30

| | |
|---|---|
| BRAND NAME | *Omega* |
| FLAVOUR | *Chicken* |
| PACKAGING |  |
| FOOD TYPE | |
| MANUFACTURER | *Omega* |
| PACK SIZE (gm) | *400gm* |
| AVAILABLE FROM | (S) (M) (P) (O) |

NOTES
*Available loose as well as packaged*

---

INSPECTOR                  *Bennett*

INSPECTOR'S COMMENTS
*As far as I was concerned this was like the
Unfinished Symphony . . .*

PAWS & CLAWS RATING

SUPPLEMENTARY REPORTS
*The Chief Inspector was asked to adjudicate on this
product as Bennett originally rated it 0. On retesting
Nutmeg and Jasmine gave it a 4. Boris and Saphi
gave both* Chicken *and* Fish *Flavour 2*

HUMAN COMMENTS
*As a dry food it seemed to make all the inspectors
thirsty*

# FOOD REPORT NO. 31
## SOUTH AFRICA

BRAND NAME            *Pamper*

FLAVOUR              *Meat with Liver*

PACKAGING

FOOD TYPE

MANUFACTURER         *Petz Products*

PACK SIZE (gm)       *410gm*

AVAILABLE FROM       (S)  (O)

NOTES
*Nutritionally balanced*

---

INSPECTOR            *Boris*

INSPECTOR'S COMMENTS
*Lovely liver . . . worth going on safari for*

PAWS & CLAWS RATING

HUMAN COMMENTS
*Boris had to be restrained from overdosing on the liver*

*The 'moggydon' factor*

# FOOD REPORT NO. 32

**BRAND NAME**    *Petcare (Gateway)*

**FLAVOUR**    *Rabbit*

**PACKAGING**

**FOOD TYPE**

**MANUFACTURER**    *Gateway Food Markets*

**PACK SIZE** (gm)    *400gm*

**AVAILABLE FROM**    (S)  *Own label variety*

**NOTES**
*Beef, Chicken and Liver flavour also available*

---

**INSPECTOR**    *Boris*

**INSPECTOR'S COMMENTS**
*This food seemed to have a high 'moggydon' factor*

**PAWS & CLAWS RATING**

**SUPPLEMENTARY REPORTS**
*Boris much preferred the* Liver *Flavour and awarded it a 4*

**HUMAN COMMENTS**
*When the Inspector is hungry he will eat anything . . . but only for so long*

# FOOD REPORT NO. 33
## SPAIN

| | |
|---|---|
| BRAND NAME | *Purina Unique Grand Cuisine* |
| FLAVOUR | *Cocktail de Frutos Del Mar* |
| PACKAGING | |
| FOOD TYPE | |
| MANUFACTURER | *Purina* |
| PACK SIZE (gm) | *100gm* |
| AVAILABLE FROM | (S)  (O) |

NOTES
*Ring-pull can. Very small quantity*

---

| | |
|---|---|
| INSPECTOR | *Lucie 'N' Flossie* |

INSPECTOR'S COMMENTS
*Olé . . . muy, muy bien!!*

PAWS & CLAWS RATING

SUPPLEMENTARY REPORTS
*Don't bother with* Continente Alimento Para Gatos –
*Nutmeg gave it a 400gm zero. If island hopping,
however, try* Majorcan Dry Purina Cat Chow Mix *which
Saphi gave a 2.* Kitekat Trozos en Salsa *from the
Canaries on the other hand was awarded a 5 plus
Spanish Crossed Whiskers by Harrods*

HUMAN COMMENTS
*Obviously better than a bullfight!*

# FOOD REPORT NO. 34

**BRAND NAME**        *Purrfect*

**FLAVOUR**           *Chicken with Salmon and Trout*

**PACKAGING**

**FOOD TYPE**

**MANUFACTURER**      *Spillers*

**PACK SIZE** (gm)    *150gm*

**AVAILABLE FROM**    (S)  (M)  (P)  (O)

**NOTES**
*Available in several other flavours*

---

**INSPECTOR**         *Arnold*

**INSPECTOR'S COMMENTS**
*This may indeed be a strange combination of flavours. However, the most memorable feature of this food is that I ate it on a Wednesday!*

**PAWS & CLAWS RATING**

**SUPPLEMENTARY REPORTS**
Choice White Fish in Prawn Jelly  *Harrods, 3*
Chicken with Salmon and Trout  *Jasmine, 2*
Lamb, Liver and Kidney  *Basil, 4*
Chicken and Turkey  *Wilkie, 2*

**HUMAN COMMENTS**
*He ate, but mainly because he was hungry*

In
MEMORIAM

HEYWOOD
He died with
his mouth full

# FOOD REPORT No. 35
## CANADA

BRAND NAME        *Purrr*

FLAVOUR           *Ragout Supreme*

PACKAGING

FOOD TYPE

MANUFACTURER      *Derby Foods*

PACK SIZE (gm)    *175gm*

AVAILABLE FROM    (S)  (O)

---

INSPECTOR         *Heywood (he died with his mouth full)*

INSPECTOR'S COMMENTS
*Keep eating, keep eating, keep eat. . .*

PAWS & CLAWS RATING *

HUMAN COMMENTS
*Heywood has now gone to the great cat basket in the sky, a very contented feline*

Cats love jelly!

# FOOD REPORT NO. 36

**BRAND NAME**      *Safeway Gourmet*

**FLAVOUR**      *Sardines in Smoked Salmon Flavoured Jelly*

**PACKAGING**

**FOOD TYPE**

**MANUFACTURER**      *Safeway*

**PACK SIZE** (gm)      *185gm*

**AVAILABLE FROM**      (S)   *Own label variety*

**NOTES**
*One of Safeway's three own label ranges*

---

**INSPECTOR**      *Teddy*

**INSPECTOR'S COMMENTS**
*This was* Love at First Bite

**PAWS & CLAWS RATING** *

Rating confirmed by Harrods, Wilkie and Arnold

**SUPPLEMENTARY REPORTS**
Safeway Cat Food: Turkey Treat *Arnold, 3*
     Fish *Teddy, 0*
Prime Cuts: Turkey *Saphi, 2*
Gourmet: Seafood Platter in Prawn Jelly *Harrods, 4*
     Mackerel *Bennett, 4*
     Tuna Flakes in Aspic *Lucie 'N' Flossie, 4*
     Chopped Beef in Gravy *Boris, 5 Crossed Whiskers*

**HUMAN COMMENTS**
*'Smaker godt', which is Norwegian for it 'tastes good'*

*Nutmeg was in heaven over the Choice White Fish*

# FOOD REPORT NO. 37

**BRAND NAME**    *Sainsbury's Supreme Selection*

**FLAVOUR**    *Beef with Liver and Kidney*

**PACKAGING**

**FOOD TYPE**

**MANUFACTURER**    *Sainsbury's*

**PACK SIZE** (gm)    *125gm*

**AVAILABLE FROM**    (S)    *Own label variety*

**NOTES**
*Supreme Selection is one of several ranges from
Sainsbury's with rather adventurous combinations.
No artificial colourings or preservatives added*

---

**INSPECTOR**    *Basil*

**INSPECTOR'S COMMENTS**
*This sounded like it was waiting for spare part
surgery!*

**PAWS & CLAWS RATING**

**SUPPLEMENTARY REPORTS**
Supreme Selection: Choice White Fish  *Nutmeg, 4*
    Turkey and Chicken  *Harrods, 2*
Supermeat: Liver  *Wilkie, 0*
    Beef  *Bennett, 1*    Chicken  *Jasmine, 2*
Supreme: Tuna  *Wilkie, 5 Crossed Whiskers*
    Salmon  *Bennett, 3*    Rabbit  *Saphi, 2*
    Beef  *Arnold, 3*    Chicken  *Wilkie, 2*

**HUMAN COMMENTS**
*Basil didn't eat it to the end*

*Sardines in Lobster Jelly*

# FOOD REPORT NO. 38

**BRAND NAME**  *St Michael's Own Choice for Cats*

**FLAVOUR**  *Beef and Kidney*

**PACKAGING**

**FOOD TYPE**

**MANUFACTURER**  *Marks & Spencer*

**PACK SIZE** (gm)  *125gm*

**AVAILABLE FROM**  (S)  *Own label variety*

**NOTES**
*Three flavours in a box of six wrappers – look like Human choc-ices. Packaging subject to change*

---

**INSPECTOR**  *Wilkie*

**INSPECTOR'S COMMENTS**
*I knew I'd had a religious experience – and then I looked at the brand name!*

**PAWS & CLAWS RATING**  *

**SUPPLEMENTARY REPORTS**
Sardines in Lobster Jelly  *Jasmine, 5*
Tuna Fish  *Bennett, 4*
Seafood in Jelly  *Harrods, 4*
Beef  *Basil, 3*
Chicken and Liver  *Boris, 4*
Chicken  *Teddy, 5 Crossed Whiskers*

**HUMAN COMMENTS**
*Expensive but obviously worth it*

# FOOD REPORT No. 39
## CANADA

BRAND NAME            *Senior Cat Food*

FLAVOUR              *Meat/Fish*

PACKAGING

FOOD TYPE

MANUFACTURER         *President's Choice*

PACK SIZE (gm)       *170gm*

AVAILABLE FROM       (S)

NOTES
*President's Choice is a Canadian range including
several 'healthy foods'*

---

INSPECTOR            *Arnold*

INSPECTOR'S COMMENTS
*An unexciting flavour belies a very acceptable repast
for a mature Feline*

PAWS & CLAWS RATING

SUPPLEMENTARY REPORTS
*President's Choice Chopped Grill rated 5 from Lucie
'N' Flossie*

HUMAN COMMENTS
*Good food for old and toothless Felines*

# FOOD REPORT NO. 40

**BRAND NAME**   *Sheba*

**FLAVOUR**   *Rabbit and Chicken*

**PACKAGING**

**FOOD TYPE**

**MANUFACTURER**   *Pedigree Petfoods*

**PACK SIZE** (gm)   *100gm*

**AVAILABLE FROM**   (S)   (M)   (P)   (O)

**NOTES**
*Available in a range of flavours*

---

**INSPECTOR**   *Harrods*

**INSPECTOR'S COMMENTS**
*Four different testings of this flavour rated between 1 and 4. I finally had to adjudicate and awarded it 3*

**PAWS & CLAWS RATING**

**SUPPLEMENTARY REPORTS**
*Wilkie gave 4 to* Beef Cuts and Kidney *(plastic pot).*
Salmon *rated 5 by Boris and 3 by Saphi, both complaining about small portion sizes.* Beef and Heart *also tested by Harrods was given a 2*

**HUMAN COMMENTS**
*Expensive for 100gm pack size*

Grams...

# FOOD REPORT NO. 41

**BRAND NAME** *Ship's Cat*

**FLAVOUR** *Tuna in Aspic*

**PACKAGING**

**FOOD TYPE**

**MANUFACTURER** *Kennelpak*

**PACK SIZE** (gm) *400gm*

**AVAILABLE FROM** (P)  (O)

**NOTES**
*Unusual and attractive label design. Ship's Cat available in a range of fish flavours in tins. This manufacturer also produces a dry food – Protein Plus in 10kg sacks*

---

**INSPECTOR** *Teddy*

**INSPECTOR'S COMMENTS**
Heaven Can Wait . . . *I'm still eating*

**PAWS & CLAWS RATING**

**SUPPLEMENTARY REPORTS**
*Harrods tested* Dry Protein Plus *and rated it a 5*

**HUMAN COMMENTS**
*Teddy originally rated this a 5, but the Chief Inspector didn't like the smell so much and downgraded it to a 4*

# FOOD REPORT NO. 42
## CANADA

**BRAND NAME**    *Slim 'n' Trim – Green Gourmet*

**FLAVOUR**    *Meat and Fish Mix*

**PACKAGING**

**FOOD TYPE**

**MANUFACTURER**    *President's Choice*

**PACK SIZE** (gm)    *411gm*

**AVAILABLE FROM**    (S)

**NOTES**
*1/3 less fat and 15% fewer calories. No artificial colours or preservatives. Low fat and specially designed for Feline fatties*

---

**INSPECTOR**    *Bennett*

**INSPECTOR'S COMMENTS**
*At last, a healthy food just for me*

**PAWS & CLAWS RATING**

**SUPPLEMENTARY REPORTS**
*See Arnold's report No. 39 on* Senior Cat Food

**HUMAN COMMENTS**
*He was over the moon about this brand, knowing that his cholesterol count would stay low!*

# FOOD REPORT NO. 43
## AUSTRALIA

BRAND NAME            *Snappy Tom*

FLAVOUR              *Tuna in Jelly*

PACKAGING

FOOD TYPE

MANUFACTURER         *Safcol*

PACK SIZE (gm)       *185gm*

AVAILABLE FROM       (S)  (M)  (O)

NOTES
*Also sold in the Middle East and other hot climates*

---

INSPECTOR            *Bennett*

INSPECTOR'S COMMENTS
*. . . Personally recommended by Ned Kelly!*

PAWS & CLAWS RATING  \*

SUPPLEMENTARY REPORTS
Snappy Tom Tropical Mackerel *from Saudi Arabia was
given 4 by Harrods and the same flavour from Jordan
was awarded 5 by Saphi.* Seafood Platter, *also from
Jordan, given a 4 by Jasmine*

HUMAN COMMENTS
*Don't they supply a Feline mouthwash?*

# FOOD REPORT NO. 44

**BRAND NAME**    *Tesco Supreme*

**FLAVOUR**    *Turkey and Chicken*

**PACKAGING**

**FOOD TYPE**

**MANUFACTURER**    *Tesco*

**PACK SIZE** (gm)    *150gm*

**AVAILABLE FROM**    Ⓢ  *Own label variety*

**NOTES**
*Other Tesco ranges include Cat Dinners, Cat Crunchies and Premium Cat Food*

---

**INSPECTOR**    *Harrods*

**INSPECTOR'S COMMENTS**
*This flavour had already received confusing ratings of 1, 2, 4 and 5. I was unable to grade it any higher than a 3*

**PAWS & CLAWS RATING**  

**SUPPLEMENTARY REPORTS**
Supreme: Beef and Chicken Livers  *Harrods, 2,*
    Mousse with Salmon and Tuna  *Lucie 'N' Flossie, 2*
Premium: Beef  *Jasmine, 2*    Salmon  *Boris, 4*
    Tuna  *Saphi, 2*

**HUMAN COMMENTS**
*Harrods was pleased to finish this assignment so that he could move on to something more adventurous*

...and temptation.

# FOOD REPORT NO. 45

**BRAND NAME**          *Top Cat Supreme*

**FLAVOUR**             *Rabbit and Liver*

**PACKAGING**

**FOOD TYPE**

**MANUFACTURER**        *Spillers*

**PACK SIZE** (gm)      *410gm*

**AVAILABLE FROM**      (S)  (M)  (P)  (O)

**NOTES**
*Small range of flavours*

---

**INSPECTOR**           *Jasmine*

**INSPECTOR'S COMMENTS**
*I can resist everything except Top Cat and
temptation . . .*

**PAWS & CLAWS RATING**

**SUPPLEMENTARY REPORTS**
Chicken and Liver *only rated 2 by Boris*

**HUMAN COMMENTS**
*Jasmine licked the bowl clean*

# FOOD REPORT NO. 46

**BRAND NAME**        *Waitrose Complete Meals for Cats*

**FLAVOUR**        *Lamb*

**PACKAGING**        *Paper sachet*

**FOOD TYPE**

**MANUFACTURER**        *Waitrose*

**PACK SIZE** (gm)        *80gm*

**AVAILABLE FROM**      (S)   *Own label variety*

**NOTES**
*Various flavours in one giant paper sack
containing 10 complete meals*

---

**INSPECTOR**        *Boris*

**INSPECTOR'S COMMENTS**
*Predictably good, but I couldn't get high on it!*

**PAWS & CLAWS RATING**

**SUPPLEMENTARY REPORTS**
Chicken *rated 3 by Basil.* Tuna *was given 2 by
Nutmeg.* Pilchard Flavour *rated 3 by Nutmeg but 0 by
Basil*

**HUMAN COMMENTS**
*Clever idea of more than one flavour in the packet –
helps the cause of adventurous eating, but Boris had
problems with the shape when crunching*

# FOOD REPORT No. 47

**BRAND NAME** — *Whiskas Select Menus*

**FLAVOUR** — *Turkey, Chicken and Bacon*

**PACKAGING** —

**FOOD TYPE** —

**MANUFACTURER** — *Pedigree Petfoods*

**PACK SIZE** (gm) — *250gm*

**AVAILABLE FROM** — (S) (M) (P) (O)

**NOTES**
*Also available in other flavours and 125gm size*

---

**INSPECTOR** — *Wilkie*

**INSPECTOR'S COMMENTS**
*Not my scene!*

**PAWS & CLAWS RATING**

**SUPPLEMENTARY REPORTS**
Sliced Liver and Beef *Basil, 1*
Turkey, Chicken and Bacon *Harrods, 2*
Lamb and Kidney *Jasmine, 4*
Beef and Chicken Livers *Boris, 2*
Salmon and Shrimp *Bennett, 3*

**HUMAN COMMENTS**
*Too expensive for something that had to be thrown out because both Wilkie and Harrods didn't like it*

# FOOD REPORT NO. 48

BRAND NAME        *Whiskas Supermeat*

FLAVOUR          *Pork and Liver*

PACKAGING

FOOD TYPE

MANUFACTURER      *Pedigree Petfoods*

PACK SIZE (gm)    *190gm*

AVAILABLE FROM    (S)  (M)  (P)  (O)

NOTES
*Ring-pull and recyclable tins. Other sizes in the*
*range are 400gm and 800gm*

---

INSPECTOR         *Harrods*

INSPECTOR'S COMMENTS
*This was serious eating, but no good for Kosher cats!*

PAWS & CLAWS RATING  *

SUPPLEMENTARY REPORTS
Plaice and Cod  *Harrods, 4 Crossed Whiskers*
Duck and Liver  *Arnold, 5 **
*Wilkie is mad about* Turkey *Flavour*

Inspectors made 43 other testings on the entire
Supermeat range. *Almost all rated between 2 and 4*

HUMAN COMMENTS
*Had to unglue his nose from the tin*

121

# DESSERTS AND TREATS

Afters?

So what's for afters? We have found a good selection of Desserts and Treats which fall into five main types. These have been tested by our Inspectors to their usual demanding standards. Reactions to snacks, treats and desserts may depend on whether you like eating between meals or prefer to wait for the serious food.

**Dry:** Very similar to main course dry food but not 'Complete'. Good for you, though, according to Bennett. The main brands are Good Girl, Thomas and Hartz which the Inspectors gave a wide range of Paws & Claws ratings. The least favourite was Good Girl Nibbles Chicken Flavour; whereas Thomas Cat Treats Beef Flavour merited a 4.

Not 'complete'

**Moist:** The only variety we could track down was Purina Lickins Beef which scored 4 – more substantial and tastier than most of the dry.

**Chewing Strips:** Thomas Kitstrips seem to have achieved the right combination of chewability, taste and smell, scoring mainly 4s. The outright winner was Rabbit Flavour which rated 5. By contrast, our Inspectors refused to eat all three flavours of Spillers Meaty Strips. (Teddy almost threatened to resign.)

**Dried fish:** All brands tested achieved similar low scores. The 'moggydon' factor set in very quickly and the Inspectors didn't like the messy way they crumbled. Basil said he'd rather wait until they brought out 'dried bird'.

**Drops and pills:** Milk drops from Good Girl and Spillers generally rated 3s or 2s. Cat Love Treats, which looked like authentic pills, did well with 5 but after careful testing and discussions a Crossed Whisker was awarded to Sherley's Top Form. The Inspectors wouldn't tell us why, but we think the yeast content had something to do with it. These treats also proved helpful in getting understandably suspicious Felines used to the idea of pills if they should ever need real medicine.

Treats are generally quite expensive but as they are mainly for fun eating, be adventurous and try them all. Boris certainly did – and look what happened to him . . .

# THE GOOD CAT FOOD GUIDE AWARDS

## GOLDEN WHISKERS AWARD FOR THE BEST UK CAT FOOD

### NOMINEES:

St Michael's Own Choice – Beef and Kidney Flavour (Wet)

Friskies Go-Cat – Lamb and Beef Flavour (Dry)

Safeway Gourmet – Sardines in Smoked Salmon Jelly (Wet)

Whiskas Supermeat – Pork and Liver (Wet)

**WINNER: SAFEWAY GOURMET – SARDINES IN SMOKED SALMON JELLY**

## HEYWOOD AWARD FOR THE BEST NON-UK CAT FOOD*

### NOMINEES:

Dokat – Fish – GERMANY (Dry)

Fido – Saumon Truite – FRANCE (Wet)

Snappy Tom – Tuna in Jelly – AUSTRALIA (Wet)

Purrr – Ragout Supreme – CANADA (Wet)

**WINNER: FIDO – SAUMON TRUITE**

*This year a new award has been included: the HEYWOOD (he died with his mouth full) AWARD for the best Non-UK Cat Food, as a mark of respect for our late colleague who went to the Great Cat Basket in the Sky.*

## GOLDEN WHISKERS AWARD FOR THE MOST ADVENTUROUS FLAVOUR COMBINATION

NOMINEES:

Duck and Liver – Whiskas Supermeat

Turkey and Heart – Spillers Kattomeat (Arthur's)

Trout and Shrimp – Felix Supreme

Chopped Pilchards in Crab Jelly – Hi Life Gourmet

***WINNER: FELIX SUPREME – TROUT AND SHRIMP***

# THE GOLDEN WHISKERS AWARD FOR THE BEST CAT FOOD OF 1992

***WINNER: SAFEWAY GOURMET – SARDINES IN SMOKED SALMON JELLY***

Be more adventurous!!

# A LAST WORD FROM THE CHIEF INSPECTOR

O ver the last twelve months, the team and I have tasted and chomped our way through well over 400 different varieties of Cat Food. Many interesting facts have come out of our combined research.

**We have all started to be adventurous eaters,** and look and feel much healthier from eating a varied diet. Before becoming Inspectors, we passively ate the same food, day in and night out. **But not any more.** Being on active duty 24 hours a day, we are willing to taste **everything** – if we don't like it, then we don't eat it, but at least we tried.

We are no longer fooled by dull, unappetising foods dressed up with fancy labels and even fancier names. If we are eating fish or meat, we prefer it to look like fish or meat and not like sludge pâté. We are also as fussy about the smell as the taste since halitosis can seriously damage our social life!

Thank you for reading the Guide. We hope that the manufacturers will also be interested in our findings. But now it is time to let you into my big secret. If I could say what I really wanted to eat, it would be **Human Food** because it is not only tasty and interesting, but freshly cooked to order!

---☆---

Dear Feline Friend

Now that you have read the Guide, we would like to make you an Honorary Inspector. Please write and tell us about Cat Foods we might have missed or any failings in our research. This will increase our knowledge and where necessary enable us to correct our assessments. Please complete and return the form below.

BRAND . . . . . . . . . . . . . . . . . . . . . . . . . . . . . . . . . . . . . . . . . .

FLAVOUR . . . . . . . . . . . . . . . . . . . . . . . . . . . . . . . . . . . . . . . . .

PACKAGING: TIN . . . . . . . . . . FOIL PACK . . . . . . . . . POT . . . . . . . . . .

BOX . . . . . . . . . SACHET . . . . . . . . . OTHER . . . . . . . . .

PACK SIZE . . . . . . . . . . . . . . . . . . . (gm)

PURCHASED FROM: SUPERMARKET . . . . . . . . . MINI-MARKET . . . . . . . . .

PETSHOP . . . . OTHER . . . .

HONORARY INSPECTOR . . . . . . . . . . . . . . . . . . . . . . . . . . . . . . . . . . .

INSPECTOR'S COMMENTS . . . . . . . . . . . . . . . . . . . . . . . . . . . . . . . . . .

. . . . . . . . . . . . . . . . . . . . . . . . . . . . . . . . . . . . . . . . . . . . . . . . . . . . .

. . . . . . . . . . . . . . . . . . . . . . . . . . . . . . . . . . . . . . . . . . . . . . . . . . . . .

. . . . . . . . . . . . . . . . . . . . . . . . . . . . . . . . . . . . . . . . . . . . . . . . . . . . .

HUMAN COMMENTS . . . . . . . . . . . . . . . . . . . . . . . . . . . . . . . . . . . . . .

. . . . . . . . . . . . . . . . . . . . . . . . . . . . . . . . . . . . . . . . . . . . . . . . . . . . .

SEND TO:    CHIEF INSPECTOR
            THE GOOD CAT FOOD GUIDE
            PO BOX 4SL
            LONDON W1A 4SL